Because I Said So!!

Parents' Guide to Parenting Teenagers

and

What's the Big Idea?!

Teenagers' Guide to the Teenage Years

© 2011 by Neal Hemmelstein
Cover and interior illustrations by Lea Wagner

Printed in the United States of America

All rights reserved. This publication is protected by Copyright, and permission should be obtained from the publisher prior to any prohibited reproduction, storage in a retrieval system, or transmission in any form or by any means, electronic, mechanical, photocopying, recording, or likewise.

Published by Eifrig Publishing, LLC
PO Box 66, 701 Berry Street, Lemont, PA 16851.
Knobelsdorffstr. 44, 14059 Berlin, Germany

For information regarding permission, write to:
Rights and Permissions Department,
Eifrig Publishing, LLC
PO Box 66, 701 Berry Street, Lemont, PA 16851, USA.
permissions@eifrigpublishing.com, 888-340-6543.

Library of Congress Cataloging-in-Publication Data

Hemmelstein, Neal
  Because I Said So!! -- What's the Big Idea?! /
  by Neal Hemmelstein, Illustrated by Lea Wagner
p.   cm.

Paperback: ISBN 978-1-936172-26-9
Ebook: ISBN 978-1-936172-27-6

   1. Psychology 2. Family Relationships
I. Hemmelstein, Neal. II. Title.

15 14 13 12 2011
5 4 3 2 1

Printed on acid-free paper. ∞

Because I Said So!!

Parents' Guide to Parenting Teenagers

and

What's the Big Idea?!

Teenagers' Guide to the Teenage Years

Neal A. Hemmelstein, Ph. D.

Eifrig Publishing LLC
Berlin   Lemont

I dedicate this book to Lois,
the best Mom I have ever met.

N. A. H.

About the Author:

Dr. Hemmelstein received his B.A. degree and elementary school teaching credential from Sonoma State University in California. He earned his M.S. and Ph.D. degrees in school psychology at The Penn State University. Dr. Hemmelstein worked as a staff psychologist at a residential treatment facility in Erie, Pennsylvania. His duties included providing inpatient and outpatient psychotherapy, staff training, and consultation, as well as oversight of the day-to-day operations of three Emotional Support classrooms. During his years in Erie, Dr. Hemmelstein also taught courses as an adjunct professor at the Behrend Campus of Penn State University to those pursuing Chemical Addiction Counseling (CAC) certification.

Between his undergraduate and graduate education, he co-founded a private elementary school (K-6) in Los Angeles, where he taught kindergarten for three years, and later taught as a clinical teacher of adolescents for two years at a private psychiatric hospital in central Pennsylvania. Dr. Hemmelstein currently lives in Lemont, Pennsylvania, where he works as a school psychologist in the State College Area School District and participates in a private group practice, Child, Adult, and Family Psychological Center, where he works with children aged five to twenty-five and their families.

TABLE OF CONTENTS

Introduction   7

Chapter One   11

Understanding is not mandatory

Your child is so much more than his/her behavior

Respect, Recognition, Appreciation

Love is learned

Chapter Two   17

Do unto others as you would have them do unto you, but don't hold your breath

Expectations provide disappointments

Consequences – natural, logical, unrelated

Be true to yourself

Resentment vs. self-honesty

Chapter Three   27

Adolescents often view themselves as invulnerable, immortal, and all-knowing. That doesn't mean they no longer need nurturance.

We cannot comprehend anything beyond our realm of experience

Reflection as a "mini-time-out"

Credit and blame are not the issue. It is all about responsibility.

Chapter Four   37

What is the goal?

Without acceptance, the work can never be complete – can never really begin

3R's: Respect for myself; Respect of another;

Responsibility for my feelings and actions

Chapter Five   47

If children drink from a fountain of love, they will grow to love themselves and others...or... Love is learned.

Everybody deserves to be loved.

Love may be unconditional, but relationship is not.

Parents' Guide

"Perhaps a child who is fussed over gets a feeling of destiny; he thinks he is in the world for something important and it gives him drive and confidence."

— Benjamin Spock

INTRODUCTION TO THE PARENT EDITION

I recently completed my guidebook for adolescents, **What's the Big Idea?!**, which you'll find by flipping this book upside-down. This physical relationship between that book and the following one acts as a metaphor for the relationship between parents and their teenage children; it can turn each other's world upside-down. (Somebody once said that parents "ruin" the first half of our life and children "ruin" the second half. Interestingly, I have shared this expression with many parents who love their children as much as you love yours, and there have rarely been strong protests.)

I wrote the teenage edition in the form of a scout reporting back to my tribe about what I have seen, tried and thought since I was their age. I suggest they use the book in the same fashion that one might use a guidebook to a foreign land. Once arrived, a traveler generally does whatever he/she likes, but in preparation for the trip, having the benefit of another's experience can help one develop a plan of one's own while avoiding some (not many) of the mistakes the writer made.

Because I Said So!!

I offer this book to you in a similar fashion, though you are further along in your journey through life than your children, and thus have much more experience from which to draw. As a result, I have little to say that you have not already thought of, experienced, heard or read about, or wondered about. However, I will present these ideas, guidelines, and wonderings in a fashion that may help you apply them to the ever challenging experience of raising, helping, and enjoying your growing and ever more capable child.

I base this guide on the assumption that we, as adults, have two responsibilities to our children beyond loving them and keeping them warm and fed:

1. I believe that teenagers (all humans, for that matter) will do whatever they like when it comes right down to the moment of taking (or not taking) action. With that in mind, our first responsibility is to equip our children with the necessary tools to live through the decisions and courses of action (or inaction) they choose to take.

2. Our second responsibility is to attempt to positively influence these decisions and courses of action (or inaction) of our children.

A powerful teaching method is teaching through modeling. I want my children to represent and stand up for the values they believe are important. That requires me to do the same. Many of my values pertain to how I treat myself, how I treat others and wish to be treated by others, and how I relate to the world around me. So, I must model these values/beliefs in my relationship with my teenagers as well as in the way I raise them and attempt to guide them.

Parents' Guide

One of the major problems parents run into with the adolescent members of their family occurs when these teenagers appear to embrace values that differ from their parents'. Our efforts to raise an independent, free-thinking, unique individual appear to blow-up in our face when this independence and uniqueness contribute to wide gaps and seemingly irreconcilable differences between our respective views of the behaviors of these no-longer-babies growing into adults of their own (if we let them live, that is!).

This is not a "How-to" book as much as a guide to developing your family's own "how-to's." Each family has its own set of values, though we often share values that others hold. I have no interest here in telling you what those values should be. I am not **your** parent so it is not for me to try to influence the decisions **you** make. I wish to share with you some of the guidelines I have discovered, observed, stumbled across, and learned the hard way during my work as a camp counselor, kindergarten teacher, teacher of adolescents in a psychiatric hospital, psychologist in a residential facility for children with behavioral, emotional, and mental health problems, school psychologist, and private practice psychologist working with children, teenagers, and families.

The ideas, thoughts, and meanderings that follow obviously reflect my own values. No one can express a thought without the influence of his/her values. I don't expect to offend anybody with the values I expose in this book, and I do not want you to think that I believe that what I have to share is without personal value. That would imply a hypocrisy I wish to avoid in all I have to say. If I am to model for you, I must take great effort at honesty with myself and honesty with you, because I ask you to do the same.

Because I Said So!!

I believe that all of us spend all of our time and efforts towards having things the way we want; all day, every day. The two primary sources of power towards having things the way you want:

Knowing how good (not "good at ...") you are.

Keeping agreements with yourself and with others.

Virtually all of the ideas, thoughts and beliefs I will share in this parent guide can be found in **What's the Big Idea?!**. That the overlap of content is so large may make it easier to share your thoughts and feelings about these chapters with your teenagers. It may help all of you develop a better understanding and more acceptance of each other in your roles as well as individuals. I have little to say to parents that I would not want teenagers to hear. You must remember that regardless of the pain, confusion, and insecurity parenthood often evokes, that no matter how much your child(ren) may **appear** to prefer an adversarial relationship with you (most teenagers would prefer to get along with their parents no matter how they act or what they say), you all are members of the same family. This includes stepparents, foster parents, guardians, or whoever takes the role of parenting. Every team has its moments of unrest and turmoil, but as the captains and coaches of your team, you provide the model that sets the tone and contributes the most to the team's ability to work together.

Parents' Guide

CHAPTER ONE

Understanding is not mandatory

Your child is so much more than his/her behavior

Respect, Recognition, Appreciation

Love is learned

Understanding is not mandatory

I will not present my ideas here in the same order as in **What's the Big Idea?!**, though I expect to touch upon all of them in the course of this guide. While none are new ideas, I discuss them here in order to apply them to how you relate with your teenager and to help you accept and enjoy, if not understand, your child.

Notice two things in the last statement. First, I said "accept and enjoy...your child." That won't always be the case when it comes to his/her behavior. We will talk more about that later. Second, I said, "if not understand your child." Understanding is a wonderful and often elusive experience. I always encourage the pursuit of understanding, but if we use it as a prerequisite to peace, pleasure, and happiness within a household of parents and adolescents, we guarantee failure. We can never know how another individual experiences the world. The more similar we are, the easier it is to guess correctly and maybe even predict future behavior based on past behavior. Parents and

Because I Said So!!

adolescents are not similar. Even when the family resemblance is "striking" and temperament of a teenager of yours "reminds me of me when I was his/her age," you are different than your child. You had different parents than your child does (I have often been identified as a master of the obvious).

Silly as it may sound, I remind you of that to assist you in recognizing the differences between you and your kid. I could go on about how different the world is today and how much more difficult it is to be a teenager today than "in our day" and blah, blah, blah to make my point of this difference, but the difference is built right into the relationship. You **can't** be a parent without having a child. Plain and simple. His/her existence brought your parentness into being (of course if you have a second child, you are a parent already before becoming another's parent).

Without parents (in the most biological sense), there could be no children. Without children, there could be no parents. This is called the parent/child dichotomy. Dichotomy is defined as "a division into two opposing parts." Each requires the other for clear definition. Dichotomies help describe and explain the world. There can be no "on" without "off;" no "up" without "down;" no "in" without "out."

Anyhow, it is this built-in "division into two opposing parts" that assures difference between you and your teenager. This difference contributes to the difficulty of gaining complete (or even partial, in some instances) understanding of your child. We, as thinking human beings, seem to need to separate in order to understand. Adolescents try to separate (literally) in order to understand the world as they try to develop

Parents' Guide

the means, knowledge, and confidence to effectively meet their needs when on their own.

Never give up on understanding your child, but don't hold it against your teenager when you don't.

Your child is so much more than his/her behavior

I made the distinction above between your child and his/her behavior. The distinction is critical. I have worked with many different children of all ages, sizes, colors, and different backgrounds and I have not met a bad one (and I have worked in places where they send "bad" kids). I have met many who exhibit behaviors I don't like, that I identify as "bad" behavior, and that cannot be accepted (harm to others or self). A person is not merely a set of behaviors. A person is much more than that. Your kids are much more than the irritating things they say or do. They are much more than the loving and love inducing things they say or do. They are unique, wonderful (you know it's true…think of how they look when they are sleeping… see, I told you they were wonderful) individuals. They deserve to be loved by you even when they are at their worst. They deserve to be loved by you even when you are at your worst.

As a kindergarten teacher, I reminded the parents that their job is to see how many different ways they can tell their children they love them. Unfortunately, teenagers often exhibit the ability to bring out the worst in their parents. The hard part is communicating that love when angry, worried, hurt, resentful, or confused. The hard part is to perceive that love when angry, worried, hurt, resentful, or confused.

Because I Said So!!

Love can be communicated while setting a limit for a teenager, it can be communicated when saying "no," it can be communicated when you are displeased. The means to this is to provide the focus of your love with three things that I believe are basic interpersonal needs: Respect, Recognition, and Appreciation.

"Love" is a powerful word. We use it in many different contexts and for many different reasons. For the purpose of explaining what I mean with regard to your relationship with your child think of "Love"= respect, recognition, and appreciation.

To explain what I mean, let's start with some dictionary definitions:

TO RESPECT– to acknowledge the existence of

TO RECOGNIZE– to identify the existence of

TO APPRECIATE– to value existence of

Another way of defining these terms:

RESPECT– I am.

RECOGNITION– I am Neal.

APPRECIATION– I am Neal and he is good.

I use the first person above because I believe that we must apply these to ourselves before we can really communicate them to others. I find it so much easier to listen to, to respond to, to show respect, recognition, and appreciation to someone I feel provides me with the same. This reintroduces the idea of modeling I mentioned earlier as a means of teaching. As well, love is learned. We must model love for our self

Parents' Guide

and love for our child in order to assist him/her in learning to love him/herself and others.

To model behavior, attitudes, views, and beliefs requires great effort and responsibility. When I do not feel respected, my first impulse is to reflect that disrespect. There have been times when I felt a lack of respect and reflected on my perception to find out later that my perception had been inaccurate. Even when that perception is accurate, reflecting disrespect only guarantees poor communication and low likelihood that the goal of that interaction will be achieved. When we do not feel our existence is acknowledged (respected), we have little motivation to please or respond as expected/requested/desired. When we do not feel our existence is identified as unique to us (recognized), we show little interest acknowledging that contact has been made with another person. When we do not feel our existence is valued (appreciated), we tend to oppose that person whom we face.

Providing respect, recognition, and appreciation, does not guarantee that another person will perceive them. Often you try your hardest to express these feelings to be met by another (your teenager, for example) who **appears** to not pick-up on, or show interest in receiving these efforts. If absent, chances approach zero of a successful interaction. When present, the likelihood of functional communication greatly increases. When living within an environment where most interactions include respect, recognition, and appreciation, they become an underlying assumption of current and future exchanges. In an environment without them, opposition becomes the major characteristic of interactions.

Because I Said So!!

I told you my ideas are not new, but rarely do we apply these guidelines to our relations with our growing children. "He/she should know I love him/her by now!" "Would I put up with this if I didn't love him/her?" "When I was a teenager... (yeah, yeah, yeah, I know, you had to know what your father wanted of you before he brought it up, and if you guessed wrong, you would not be allowed to eat or breathe for a week. Oh yeah, and don't forget that 5-mile hill you had to climb (both ways) to get to school...in the snow...everyday...in the dark...with a cast on your leg...while carrying your little sister on your back.)."

People don't often talk about respect by an adult for a child. We always hear about the demand for respect by a child for an adult. We also have experienced the ol' "Do as I say not as I do" school of thought. It is the easiest route, and even though we all remember how ineffective it was when our folks tried it on us, we still can be found hiding behind it when all else fails, or when we can think of nothing else.

I have introduced respect, recognition, and appreciation, but how does one apply such lofty views of functional relationship with this being who seems to have so little in common with you? No easy task. I will discuss next what it takes to apply this stuff.

Parents' Guide

Chapter 2

Do unto others as you would have them do unto you, but don't hold your breath

Expectations provide disappointments

Consequences – natural, logical, unrelated

Be true to yourself

Resentment vs. self-honesty

Do unto others as you would have them do unto you, but don't hold your breath.

In case you didn't notice, I have just described behavior based upon the Golden Rule: **Do unto others as you would like them to do unto you.** I referred to it as "modeling." I place it in contrast to "Do as I say, not as I do." The rub comes when you attempt to model and "do unto…" and your model is not reflected in another's behavior. Teenagers will wait you out, force you to match their behavior, which you perceive as absent of respect, recognition, or appreciation. There is only so much you can take before you lash out toward your child in a similar fashion. You no longer listen, you no longer appear to care about their feelings, you no longer remember how valuable your child is. Your feelings are real, as are your child's. You are not bad because you react this way. You are a human being with interpersonal needs of your own.

Because I Said So!!

Following the Golden Rule is not easy. Strict interpretation of this guideline will test anyone's patience and the expectation of another person (your teenage offspring, in particular) to reflect your model can be a set-up. In fact, what often happens to me is that in my frustration, I abandon my attempts at providing a model and adopt the behavior, posture, position, and tactics of my partner in a particular interaction. So, they are now providing the model and I am doing unto them as I don't like them to do unto me. Sound familiar?

You may have started out calm and respectful in your effort to communicate with your child, but were immediately greeted by insolence, lack of attention or apparent interest, and even anger from where, you do not know. After facing that repeatedly or after a difficult day of your own, you may find yourself going toe to toe with your child, attempting to outdo his/her disrespect, lack of recognition or appreciation. The Golden Rule becomes the farthest thing from your mind, as you battle with your child and yourself, trying to control your own aggressive and possibly violent impulses.

In an attempt to help you with this, I have added something to the Golden Rule: Do unto others as you like them to do unto you, **but don't hold your breath!** The trap in the practice of the Golden Rule is the expectation that your behavior/actions will be reflected/reciprocated simply because you provided the model. It doesn't often work that way, does it? However, lack of immediate reflection of your model does not mean providing that model is a waste of time or effort. Providing a model simply allows you to ask for the same. It does not allow you to **expect** it.

Parents' Guide

Expectations provide for disappointments

Expectations are a particularly difficult area for parents, because on the one hand, it sets us up for failure, but on the other hand, parents must have some expectations of their children's behavior as a means of guiding their children's development. It is reasonable for a parent to expect a 5-year-old to put away toys at the end of playing with them in the family room, so others can use the room next. But do we expect the same of a 2-year-old? Must they do it entirely on their own, all the time? What is the appropriate expectation? It is reasonable to expect your child to tell you where he/she will be, but is it reasonable to expect them to like it when you want them home sooner than they wish to return?

It is reasonable to expect your children to keep agreements they have made with you, but how do you respond when the agreement is not kept? What consequences are established for not keeping an agreement? And shouldn't the consequences be matched to the incident rather than a mandatory punishment for any infraction resembling a broken agreement? Expectations and when to have them, combined with emotions (yours and your child's), make parenting more of an art than a science.

Guidelines are valuable, but children change so quickly, and as they develop, expectations must change with them. And every situation is different. A child coming home a half-hour late without a phone call from an "away" high school football game across the county is different than returning a half-hour late without a phone call from a friend's house down the street. When are expectations necessary? When do they set us up?

Because I Said So!!

If I had set answers for each of these situations, I would write a manual simply listing situations with accompanying expectations and appropriate consequences. Set answers to these situations imply that each is identical, that there is one answer to each question, which a cookbook with recipes for all occasions could suffice. It just isn't so.

Expectations change as a child matures. The idea of expectation (to require something of somebody) remains constant, however. As parents, we must accept our attachment to that requirement. The importance we place in that expectation directly affects how we react/feel when that expectation is not met. Our expectations of our children require a frequent revisiting in order to keep them current with regard to your own needs as well as with the needs of your teenager.

It may be true that in the past your 15-year-old always enjoyed visiting your older brother and his wife and family for a Sunday together. Now he would prefer to not miss his Sunday band practice. You only visit your brother on 4 or 5 Sundays a year. How important is it for your boy to go with you every time you visit? That same adolescent may also feel like he no longer needs to eat dinner with the rest of the family. He would rather watch the television while he eats. How important is it for him to sit at the dinner table with you? You must decide. You must be honest with yourself in making those decisions and maintaining a consistent position (consistency does not preclude flexibility).

Your values, what is important to you, comes into play with honest representation of your expectations of your children's behavior. If you want your child to stand up for what he/she believes is right, then you have a responsibility to do the same. Modeling again rears its ugly head!!

Parents' Guide

It may appear that raising an independent thinker is only asking for trouble when they become teenagers. Suddenly (or so it seems) your teenager no longer appears to embrace the sense of family that you associate with visiting your brother. The same may apply to his lost interest in sharing the evening meal with his own household. Does he need to go with you every time you visit your brother? Must he sit at the dinner table with his parents and siblings? The answer may be different for each of those questions and for each family, and that these answers may be different does not imply any contradiction. Everybody's needs must be considered, and made clear, to contribute to effective action/interaction.

Adolescence is a time of life when friends often appear to be the most important thing. This can get in the way if parents deny that. This realization may help you make some adjustments for some expectations, but not for others. When considering the 2 examples I have used, it may be acceptable (though a bit disappointing) not to take your teenager **every** time you visit your brother. However, it may not be acceptable to you for your teenager to eat separately from the rest of the family on any regular basis.

Remember, if you stand up for what you believe: a) you must be willing to accept responsibility for the difficulties that accompany that position; and b) your child will likely become an adult who stands up for what he/she believes. Resolving situations such as these requires honesty with yourself and those involved and respect, recognition, and appreciation of yourself and those involved. Keeping those things in mind will enhance your ability to remain consistent, though flexible.

Because I Said So!!
Consequences – natural, logical, unrelated

The idea of consequences, on the other hand, can be presented in a more general fashion. Consequences are best used and enforced when they pertain to the behavior and the situation in which the behavior was involved.

Consequences should not be confused with punishment. Punishment teaches a child what not to do, not what to do (This information was borrowed with permission from "Parenting: A Skills Training Manual" by Louise Guerney, Ph.D.; 1995; Relationship Press.). There are other limitations to punishment:

A. Children learn to avoid communicating with those who punish them.

B. Children may stop a behavior when the punisher is present but resume that same behavior when the punisher is absent.

C. The more a punishment is used, the less effective it becomes. The punisher is forced to resort to harsher and harsher punishment.

D. Parents who use physical punishment serve as a model for physical aggression.

Natural consequences are those that occur naturally as a result of some action or inaction. They often are the best, but not always available. EX: If the child is late for dinner, he/she eats a cold dinner or has the responsibility for making it hot if he/she wants.

Logical consequences are those that you must impose upon the child but which have direct connection with the broken limit. If a child leaves his ipod on the back step after he has been told to bring it inside, you

Parents' Guide

could leave it there to get rained upon and ruined as a natural consequence. But you (or your teenager) paid a lot of money for it and you are not prepared to allow the natural consequences to prevail. A logical consequence might be to impose a restriction on the use of the ipod for a prescribed amount of time or taking the device yourself and putting it away until your child looks for it at which time the two of you can discuss when or how the ipod will be returned. It is much easier for the teenager to make the connection and accept the consequence between leaving his ipod and a related consequence than it would be for him/her to make the connection between this act of forgetfulness (I know you, in your anger, are prone to view it as irresponsibility, but that simply is an indulgence of judgment rather than an assessment) and an unrelated consequence like being grounded for the weekend.

Unrelated consequences are those you impose as a last resort when natural or logical consequences haven't worked or none can realistically be imposed. Even when using unrelated consequences, however, don't go overboard with the punishment. Remember that you are trying to teach the child to master a behavior on his/her own, and that a punishment that is too harsh or hard to enforce may defeat your purpose. The child is likely to remember only the extreme punishment, not that he/she should follow the rule.

Be true to yourself

I mentioned the idea "Do unto others as you like them to do unto you, **but don't hold your breath"**

Because I Said So!!

earlier. I must balance that with another idea I link it to when I speak to your child in the other half of this book. Be true to yourself! This can be very confusing to anyone, let alone a parent who recognizes the sacrifices sometimes necessary to make for your children. What I tell the kids is that if you would sell out yourself, you will sell out your best friend. They always think I am hitting below the belt with that one until I cite the following examples: You and a friend are both running for an elected office, you vote for your friend and you lose by one vote. If you choose not to vote for yourself, how can you ask anyone else to vote for you? You see your Mom across the street with hands full with bags of groceries. In your interest in helping you hurriedly cross the street without looking and get hit by a car. How much use are you then to your mother?

One of the difficulties with being true to yourself in the guise of a parent is discerning where you stop and your child begins. That distinction blurs easily for someone who carried this being for nine months before making his/her presence felt by anybody else. It gets hard to define those limits of selfness when you have slept on the floor by the crib because your infant was experiencing breathing problems and you could not sleep unless you could hear his/her breathing. It is impossible for your teenager to understand that and you must recognize that there is no contradiction between being true to yourself and feeling that your child is a part of you. I did not say it was easy or simple, just that it is not a contradiction.

Parents' Guide

Resentment vs. self-honesty

I mentioned earlier about the importance of reflecting your values in all of your actions to encourage the same in your child. Being true to yourself is not synonymous with selfishness. It simply refers to self-honesty. Remember, all your feelings are real. If you deny the feelings now, you will live to resent the person later for whom you denied them. Your feelings are separate from your actions, though they influence each other. Certainly in the course of parenthood there are times when you choose to sacrifice, give up, put off activities, events, experiences because of the presence of your child and his/her needs/wants/wishes. Those are the rules and I appreciate your ability/willingness to look to your child's welfare/interests/desires before you make your own plans. It's the pretense to yourself that you don't mind, you don't care, it doesn't matter that will turn around and bite you.

Resentment is insidious. A little resentment doesn't seem to make a difference. "She's only a kid." "I didn't really want to do that anyway." "It was stupid of me to think I could…" Resentment acts on our psyche as a heavy metal (e.g., lead, aluminum) can act upon our physical body. Heavy metals in minute quantities may not harm us; however, heavy metals remain in our body to accumulate over time. While a little bit now may not hurt, a little bit now, a little bit later, and a little bit more after that, etc. can result in a toxic level causing harm, discomfort, even death. Resentment works in the same fashion. A little bit now doesn't seem to be an unworthy exchange for keeping a child happy. But not unlike the heavy metals, over time resentment can poison a relationship (this does not pertain only to parent/child relationships). Once

Because I Said So!!

it reaches that toxic level it becomes increasingly difficult to want to show respect, recognition, appreciation to another, let alone serve that person.

You have a responsibility to your child to acknowledge these feelings, though not necessarily to your child. You must acknowledge them to yourself (by means of sharing with your mate, friend, or counselor, or writing them down, or whatever means you have developed for such a purpose) and own them so they don't stick and become seeds of resentment. If for no other reason, I throw the ol' "modeling" reason up at you. You do not want your child to have unresolved feelings festering within to negatively affect their view of themselves or their relationships, now, do you?

This task I describe to you opens the door for guilt to enter. "How could I be so selfish?" The trouble with guilt is that it resolves little for any length of time. It is a good, in-the-moment ameliorative (like aspirin when you think you may have broken your finger), but it does not remove the source of the discomfort. I read somewhere that described guilt as a currency we use. When we have paid enough of this currency we repeat whatever it is over which we experienced guilt.

You must remember that you are a human with feelings who needs respect, recognition, appreciation, just like your child. Minimizing resentment allows the sacrifices to be less trouble, the delay of gratifying your desires less troublesome, the changing of your plans less depressing. (Do you know how to make God laugh? Tell God you have plans.) If you were not a human it would be so much easier to be a parent. However, if you were not a human, you would not be able to model for your child what it is like to be one.

Parents' Guide

Chapter Three

Adolescents often view themselves as invulnerable, immortal, and all-knowing. That doesn't mean they no longer need nurturance.

We cannot comprehend anything beyond our realm of experience

Reflection as a "mini-time-out"

Credit and blame are not the issue. It is all about responsibility.

Adolescents often view themselves as invulnerable, immortal, and all-knowing. That doesn't mean they no longer need nurturance.

In case you hadn't noticed, teenagers often have a different (from yours) view, assessment, belief of their capabilities, vulnerability, mortality. Their life experience has consisted of a meteoric growth in their skills, in number as well as level. Ten years ago, they might not have yet learned to ride a bicycle. Now they have just received their driver's license. Everyday, or every month, anyhow, they have grown a bit taller, stronger, smarter. There is every indication, to them, based upon their own experience of themselves that this rate of increase in these areas will continue at the same rate.

That's pretty heady stuff. That does not excuse them from responsibility for exhibiting poor judgment

27

Because I Said So!!

with regard to their capacity to hurt themselves, to make mistakes, to act without thought or review of potential consequences. It may help understand it better, however. They are not nearly as old as they think they are, but consider from whence they came!

We cannot comprehend anything beyond our realm of experience

To our kids , 16 years is their whole life! That's a long time. To them, they are already 16. To us, they are "only" 16. We have the backdrop of 35 or more years to compare 16 years as a short time. Do you remember attempting to prevent pain or possible injury from fire/extreme heat by simply talking to your 1-, 2-, 3-, 4-year-old? How'd that go?!

That's what I mean by "We cannot comprehend anything beyond our realm of experience." They can't "know" that they are "only" 16 years old. That is a difficult idea to grasp and can be quite frustrating when trying to reason with a teenager. They speak and think so well and based on their experience, they have evidence that something they could not do before they can do now. They project that experience upon their plan making, decision-making, and action taking. "I never had problems learning how to handle my bicycle at ever increasing speeds and degrees of difficulty. I always saw the need to slow down before I rode too fast and rarely fell off." Ergo, "I can handle anything a car has to offer with regard to speed, danger, stimulation." As well, pushing limits (e.g., Mom/Dad letting go of the bicycle seat while running along side a new bike rider) is how we see for ourselves our true capacities. That is the logic a teenager uses.

Parents' Guide

Again, I don't present this as a rationale to abdicate your responsibilities for setting limits on and providing guidance in your child's decision-making. As I said in the introduction, teenagers will do whatever they want when it comes right down to the moment of taking (or not taking) action. I go on to say that our responsibilities are to equip our children with the necessary tools to live through the decisions and courses of action (or inaction) they choose to take and to attempt to influence the decisions made and courses of action (or inaction) taken by our children. But the rub comes in with the realization that we can't tell them something they don't already know. That presents the greatest complication in performing the duties of a parent, because your adolescent will not understand or appreciate where you are coming from when you set a particular limit, consequence, and/or rule.

A friend of mine called me after her 14-year-old son had come home at 3 am, without calling her, when he was due home at midnight on a particular Friday night. Her son, a bright, loving boy, had no understanding of his mother's worry, fear and anger over his overdue arrival. He assured her that he was "only" at a buddy's house, watching movies. That if it were okay for him to be there until midnight, what was the big deal about coming home 3 hours later? He was a bit indignant about that seemingly irrational position his mother took. His mother introduced the idea to him that she needed to know that he is safe and unharmed. He responded with the clear evidence (his presence at that moment): "See, I'm fine. Why are you so bent out of shape?" This late hours discussion lasted a couple of hours. My friend reported that she felt at the end of the discussion, her son was able to

Because I Said So!!

accept (if not understand) that she will always have the need to know that he is safe and unharmed. She was able to acknowledge to herself and to him that her growing faith in him and his ability to take care of himself will ease the degree of reaction and worry over his well being, but that it will never disappear. He, not yet having the experience of parenthood, can only believe her. He cannot "know" what she means.

Developmentally, teenagers are busily working on independence and differentiation from their parents. Their size, verbal abilities, and belief in their right to do anything they want or feel capable of doing often obscure to themselves as well as to their parents their needs for nurturance. Not only that, they often do everything they can to push us away, hurt our feelings, and assure us that all they need are the keys to the car and the freedom to come home whenever they want. This can often set the tone for the relationship you share with your child. When feeling unappreciated, ignored, disrespected, and viewed as an unnecessary evil, you can be hard pressed to want to embrace (literally and figuratively) your adolescents, remind them how wonderful they are, and/or how glad you are to have them around (not always easy to keep in touch with when feeling disabused by an apparently thoughtless, heartless individual). Nurturance as a form of interaction is the furthest thing from your mind.

I taught kindergarten for three years before working as a teacher of adolescents in a psychiatric hospital. My kindergartners taught me the benefit and importance of nurturing and communicating to them how much I valued them. Actually, being 5- and 6-year-olds, they made it easy. We adults find young children appealing. We often refer to our response

Parents' Guide

to them as "wanting to eat them up" with the expression of our love for and interest in them.

Teenagers, on the other hand, often do all they can to repel us, push us away, make themselves unappealing to us. Before my work in the psychiatric hospital, I had only worked with elementary school-aged children. I entered the classroom filled with eighteen 12- to 18-year-olds and in little time I was blasted by many of them. They immediately challenged my authority, called me names, and did all they could to deliver the message that I was not welcome, I was not worthy of their respect, and that I was significantly interfering with how they spent their time in my classroom.

Having gotten my practical experience from kindergartners, I only had the skills, tools, and experiences with which they had provided me. I had no choice but to use what I knew in my efforts to learn this new role as a teacher of adolescents. That I was new to this group as well as to the characteristic behaviors described above, I was able to not take affect (not take personally, not have my feelings hurt, not get angry and yell at them). I did not react to this onslaught of attempted abuse and they quickly gave it up, much to my surprise and great relief. I offered the same nurturance I provided my kindergartners and received similar results from my new teenage charges. Teenagers have lived longer, spoken longer, and think and talk faster than 5-year-olds, but their needs for attention, nurturance, and reflection (see Chapter One on respect, recognition, appreciation) remain as great or greater than when they were 5 years old.

Your feelings are real, as are those of your teenager. Teenagers have the remarkable skill to know and

Because I Said So!!

frequently "push your buttons." They know just how often to complain about the same thing, how long to ignore you, how impatient and unappreciative to be to get you angry, how to hurt your feelings, how to question your authority and tap into your insecurity around your parenting. Our impulse and tendency (as the humans we are) is to respond in kind, to yell, and/or "show him/her who's boss." However, we know how unrewarding, ineffective, and regrettable acting out of anger, fear, and/or insecurity generally are.

Providing yourself with your own "time-out" at these moments can allow you to regain awareness of your feelings (often when strong feelings overtake us, we are not even aware that they have done so) and, in turn, better serve yourself, your child, and the situation at hand. When things get really heated, it may be best to literally designate neutral corners for you and your kid to go to in order to allow the wave of strong feelings to pass and allow for control of your behavior to return and the awareness of the present moment to return (vs. all the old feelings and unresolved situations in the past that so resemble the current one). Make a date to reconvene in 10 minutes (or a half hour or tomorrow morning) to resolve things.

Reflection as a "mini-time-out"

Something else that can provide you with a brief "time-out," long enough to prevent you from acting out of anger, etc. is called "reflection." Reflection refers to assisting the person with whom you are interacting in identifying how he/she may be feeling

Parents' Guide

at that moment. That does not mean saying, "What are you so angry about?" or "That's so childish to get upset about something like that." Reflection refers to providing a verbal mirror of what your teenager appears to be feeling. "You are angry." "You must be really disappointed that…" "You don't think it is fair that…"

Reflection communicates two very powerful messages: 1) It helps an individual identify his/her own feelings (I have been in discussion with someone when they say to me, "What are you so angry about?" and I yell at them, "I'm not angry!!!!" Oops, I guess I was and didn't even know it); 2) "You must be paying attention to me if you know how I feel." That can be very soothing and may contribute to short-circuiting the snowballing feelings he/she may be experiencing.

Reflection can be very powerful. It can replace responding in kind ("You yell at me, I'll yell at you"); one-upsmanship ("You yell at me, I will yell at you louder"); or empty threats ("You must…or else!). There are numerous other irrational and ineffective ways we respond when we feel very angry. The nature of passion is that in the midst of it we do not think very well. If nothing else, reflection in the midst of a heated, unpleasant, irritating interaction with your kid can give you that "time-out" I mentioned above.

And you do not have to worry about being wrong with your reflection. We only have another's behavior to guess how he/she feels if they are not verbally expressing it. There are no dangers in inaccurately reflecting. Reflecting anger when someone is just confused won't prompt anger. In fact, reflecting the wrong feeling may result in the person correcting

Because I Said So!!

you, and in turn, becoming aware of him/herself- the goal of reflection.

The purpose of a time-out when we impose it upon a child is not to punish him/her, but to provide that person with a few minutes to gather him/herself, to regain self-control, to return to the present (rather than stuck, like an old vinyl long-play record with a skip in it, unable to move on). Reflection can give you that same opportunity–the opportunity to regain awareness of yourself. That can prevent you from acting out of anger or fear, something we usually regret later and generally is not terribly effective, anyway.

Credit and blame are not the issue. It is all about responsibility.

Your feelings are real, as are your teenager's. Your feelings (or your teenager's feelings) are not an excuse for behavior. They may be the reason for actions, but they are not excuses. You (and your child) are so much more than your feelings and/or your behavior. Regardless of the reasons for your feelings and actions, or your feelings and actions themselves, we all remain responsible for all of our actions and feelings. That is different from blame or credit for one's actions and feelings.

I think of blame as identifying an individual (or self) as "bad" because of having done something "bad." I think of credit as identifying an individual (or self) as "good" because of having done something "good." That individual (or you) is always good, nonetheless.

Parents' Guide

If I, as a starting member of a basketball team in a championship game, make a shot at the final buzzer to win the game, I am not "good" because I made it. I am already good. I wouldn't have been on the court if I weren't good. If I miss that same shot to lose the game, I am not "bad" because I missed it. I am already good. I wouldn't have been on the court if I weren't good. I am responsible (able to respond). I am always good. You are always good. Your child is always good. There are certainly behaviors and methods of expressing feelings that may be unacceptable, unwarranted, even "bad." And each of us is responsible. Credit and blame only confuse things and imply that we are merely our feelings and actions.

Because I Said So!!

Parents' Guide

Chapter Four

What is the goal?

Without acceptance, the work can never be complete – can never really begin

3R's: Respect for myself; Respect of another;

Responsibility for my feelings and actions

What is the goal?

I believe there is merit in beginning every problem-solving process or any endeavor, for that matter, with "What is the goal?".

Unless we know what we wish to accomplish, achieve, complete, gain, receive, we cannot really begin working toward it. Rarely one to quote from songs (it can be so sappy), I choose to now. "How can I go forward when I don't know which way I am facing?" is from a John Lennon song off of his **Imagine** album. I heard it first as a freshman in college, a time when I was lost and impressionable, which may explain why it stuck.

We must identify, honestly, what our goal as parents is, in order to provide us with guidance and direction in our parenting. I believe that the goal of parenting is to assist a child, by means of communicating and modeling our love for them, in becoming whoever he/she wishes to become. That may seem

Because I Said So!!

a little corny or pie-in-the-sky and may not be yours, but you need to know the underlying assumption of this whole book. I will get to that shortly.

At a more practical and practicable level there is value in asking that question of yourself at the beginning of every interaction you have with your teenager. In case you haven't noticed, an effective means your teenager may use to avoid addressing issues is to confuse you or distract you or help you forget what your purpose at that moment may have been. As well, in the heat of the moment we unconsciously change the goal or forget it. Part of my personal work is to ask myself that question as often as I can remember, "What is the goal?"

One summer afternoon, as a ten-year-old, I found myself at the top of the stairs (we lived in a 2-story house with the bedrooms upstairs) and did not know why I had climbed the stairs. I paused for a moment and unable to figure out what brought me there, I turned around and descended. As I reached the bottom of the stairs, I was able to see out the front door (it was summer, the door was open with a screen door) and there was my friend, Brad, pounding his baseball mitt. I had gone upstairs to get my own mitt to have a catch with him. I turned around, again climbed the stairs and grabbed my mitt that was in my bedroom.

I had forgotten my goal. Because I was 10 years old, I feel comfortable in not attributing it to senility. As an overweight child, I was out of breath and not happy that I had to climb those steps twice in order to get what I want (achieve my goal). A simple, and maybe silly example, but have you ever observed

Parents' Guide

yourself do something similar? That's what I thought.

I wrote earlier about how our ability to think is often impaired when in the grips of strong emotion or passion. What also can occur at those moments is our forgetting or replacing the goal. What may have started out as a discussion about developing a schedule for the upcoming weekend (where you are taking him/her and when; what time everyone is due home; who will do what) turns into a shouting match. The original goal, developing a schedule, gets supplanted by the goal of making sure he/she knows who is in charge or who is right or explaining the values you embrace. All of those may be valuable goals to address, but are they the ones you had originally set out to achieve at that moment? If we can remember what the goal is, we can better address ourselves to the most effective means of achieving that particular goal. If I forget it or replace it in mid-stream, then "How can I go forward when I don't know which way I am facing?" (Sorry!)

Identifying your goal for your adolescent at the beginning of the interaction will help you remember it. It will help him/her know why you feel the need to take up their valuable time and attention ("Can I go now?" he/she asks in impatience, disdain and a roll of the eyes). It also provides the opportunity for both of you to determine whether or not that goal can be shared. You know all too well, I am sure, that nothing ever gets accomplished, completed, or resolved when our partner in goal achievement has a different goal or misunderstands our goal or refuses to accept it as the goal. There are times that modification of the goal may enhance

Because I Said So!!

its likelihood of being shared, and then, achieved. Identifying your goal up-front allows for a review and modification and consensus (For example: initial goal is for your teenager to spend time with his/her visiting grandparents on Saturday afternoon of the only weekend they will be around. An alteration to that goal that may facilitate accomplishment of that goal might be: to spend a few hours with the grandparents sometime between Thursday night, when they arrived and Monday morning when they leave.) Willingness to alter a goal does not mean you are "giving in." It does not mean you are not "in charge." It does not mean you are "spoiling" him/her ("Why, when I was a kid…!"). It means you are interested in achieving the goal and showing respect, recognition, and appreciation for your child. (Shared in Chapter 1 are my beliefs about the importance, power, and value of respect, recognition, and appreciation).

Without acceptance, the work can never be complete – can never really begin

I mentioned earlier in this chapter that the primary goal of parenting is to assist a child in becoming whoever he/she wishes to become. This often is much easier to remember when the child is young, endearing, and receptive to your ideas, values, and to meeting your needs. A necessary and valuable quality in an individual, and one we claim to nourish and encourage is independent thought. "Think for yourself!" "If he/she told you to jump off a bridge, would you do it?" And so on. Yes, independent thinking is valuable and important in becoming

Parents' Guide

who we wish to become. While we like it when we observe independent thinking in our children, we do not like it when that independent thought happens to be different from ours. Oops!

Battles over values and "right" behavior and how our teenager will display them are frequent – and sometimes seemingly unending. Sometimes the kid's position is a position of convenience; sometimes it is a position just to be contrary; sometimes it is an honest reflection of the adolescent's feelings, views, beliefs. Adolescence is a time for differentiation and separation from parents. Disagreement and questioning are natural means for an individual to build one's own world view and relationship to one's world. Simply discounting these efforts (yelling, complaining, opposing and defying) and reacting to them in kind will serve no one and will likely push the teenager away and discourage him/her from sharing these thoughts and ideas.

Please do not interpret the last sentence to mean that avoiding confrontation or disagreement is the goal. What is important and necessary in any relationship is the acceptance of the other for who he/she is. Acceptance of oneself is a prerequisite of accepting another, as well. If you truly want your child to stand up for what he/she values or thinks is "right," you must model that for them. I do not ask you to give up your standards of behavior when I suggest accepting your child. I encourage you to make those standards clear and hope that you can re-evaluate them on an ongoing basis. The toughest part about being a parent is that once you get the hang of taking care of an eleven-year-old, he/she turns twelve, bringing a higher level of skills

Because I Said So!!

development and more skills. This requires a constant re-assessment of our expectations of our children and our standards of behavior. That is not synonymous with "giving in." It does require knowing and accepting what your needs are along with accepting your teenager and his/her behavior. "Accept" means respecting, recognizing, and evaluating your kid in the moment, not "letting him/her get away with it." It provides two things. It sends an important and sometimes very soothing message, "You exist and I am glad." It also provides you with good and current information regarding your adolescent and what he/she is doing. When we simply react to or invalidate ("That's the stupidest thing I have ever heard!"; "Why would you want to do that?!"; "If I had tried that when I was a kid, my father would have killed me!") a teenager's position, behavior, or feelings, we have then guaranteed an unpleasant and unsatisfying resolution to the situation at hand. We will also discourage them from even bothering to share anything with us. Would you continue to discuss changes in your job description with someone who dismissed you before you completed a sentence or countered any suggestion with, "You've got to be kidding!"?

You are in charge **and** your child has power. If you disallow that power by means of not accepting who they are and what they want and what they have to say, you discourage them from bothering to ask in the first place. It's much easier to ask forgiveness than it is to ask permission. And your child will avoid you at the front end (asking permission) if they do not feel heard or accepted. They will just hope they don't get caught and if they do, they will

Parents' Guide

apologize afterwards. They will believe that their power is in being in charge and will make you and themselves miserable misusing their power by trying to usurp the "in charge" role you hold as the parent.

I mentioned earlier in this chapter of the need to accept yourself as an important component to parenting. Again, do not equate acceptance with a giving up of standards. Personally, I have subscribed (though not proud to admit it) to the method of beating myself up when I make a mistake, do something "wrong" or "bad." The belief behind that position is that if punished or hurt as a result of my error (poor performance, etc.), I won't do it again. I have no evidence that it actually serves the alleged purpose of preventing the same mistake (choice) in the future, but I continue to indulge in that method. How about you? Is that how you would like your child to act towards him/herself?

Imagine your child coming home from school with a "D" on a test in a class in which he/she usually does well. And didn't even study for it. Would you want your child to berate him/herself, call him/herself names, ignore what contributed to the error, or cause physical harm to him/herself or someone else? I didn't think so. If you model that behavior directed inward to yourself or react that way to your child's behaviors, choices, actions, you will see the same method employed by your child. Modeling is a subtle and very powerful teaching tool. How you treat yourself influences how your child treats him/herself and likely resembles how you treat your child.

Because I Said So!!

3R's:

Respect for myself
Respect of another
Responsibility for my feelings and actions

The 3R's (no, not Reading, 'Riting and 'Rithmetic) provide simple, if not easy guidelines for how to treat yourself. This complements and supplements respect, recognition, and appreciation. The 3R's consist of:

Respect for yourself.
Respect for others.
Responsibility for your actions and feelings.

Using the definition for "respect" that I identified earlier, "the acknowledgement of," and recognizing that "responsibility" refers to "the ability to respond" may help.

It is vital to acknowledge yourself. This refers to and requires self-honesty and making the effort to make your needs known.

If we do not acknowledge others, how can they know (perceive?) we know they are out there? Have you ever noticed how annoying or hurtful or disappointing it can be when you say hello to somebody and they do not respond in any fashion? We wonder: "Do they know I'm here?" "What's their problem?" "Do they wish I weren't here?" "Don't they like me anymore?" When we "wonder" these questions, it implies that we don't "know" the answers. When we don't "know" the answers to these questions, we are far less likely to share, cooperate, or work with them.

Our ability to respond communicates to others that we do, indeed, respect them and ourselves.

Parents' Guide

Implementation of the 3R's contributes directly to the process of identification and achievement of a shared goal, whatever that goal may be.

Goal achievement between two people requires sharing, cooperation and working together. Each person must practice the 3R's for each to "know" the other is interested in and capable of achieving an identified goal. The only way we can ask the other to institute their 3R's is to model them for him/her in ourselves.

Adding the 3R's to the Golden Rule (but don't hold your breath) and respect, recognition, and appreciation completes the "indications" that serve us in our efforts to live through and enjoy our adolescent(s). I prefer the word "indications" to the word "rules." "Rules" imply a clear "right" and "wrong" which feeds into judgment (of self and others) of "good" and "bad." And you (you, your child) are always good (remember?). "Indications" imply guidelines; what will help achieve a given goal. The goals of parenting, as I identified in the Introduction are:

1. to equip our children with the necessary tools to live through the decisions and courses of action (or inaction) they choose to take.

2. to attempt to influence the decisions made and courses of action (or inaction) taken by our children.

And while working toward those goals, these three ideas will also assist you in accepting and enjoying, if not fully understanding, your child.

Because I Said So!!

The Parent Handbook

Chapter Five

If children drink from a fountain of love, they will grow to love themselves and others....
Or... Love is learned.

Everybody deserves to be loved.

Love may be unconditional, but relationship is not.

If children drink from a fountain of love, they will grow to love themselves and others....Or... Love is learned.

If Love is the answer, what was the question, again?

The previous chapters attempted to provide you with a practical view of love in action. I know I stated in the introduction that this book was to be a guide for parents "beyond loving them..." I am not sure I believe there is really anything "beyond loving them," but it makes it difficult to talk about and helps little if I merely stated: All you need to do is love your child to be assured you are doing the "right" thing. That is like saying: "All you need to be a good basketball player is to play good basketball."

I have attempted to break down the idea of communicating your love for your child into some practical guidelines, ideas, and suggestions for action. A thread throughout the previous chapters is the idea of modeling. I discussed it in various ways. The most

Because I Said So!!

important and powerful model to provide is that of respecting recognizing, and appreciating yourself and your child. Love is learned. If children drink from a fountain of love, they will grow to love themselves and others.

Love is learned

Our ability to love another is limited only by our ability to love ourselves. We learn to love by the model our parents provided in their love of us. We apply that model to loving ourselves, upon which time we can love another. Only when we respect, recognize and appreciate ourselves can we receive or provide another's respect, recognition, and appreciation.

All of us have these less than perfect models (our parents' love of us) because our parents are humans and had parents who were limited by the level of love they had for themselves. And on and on through the generations. That is not to say that children cannot come to love themselves more than their parents loved themselves; it is just a slow, if any, improvement across the generations. "They" say it takes 3 generations of the absence of physical (or sexual) abuse to remove it from a family system. So, our parents' self-love (or absence of) is not a limit to our self-love, it is simply a very strong influence. I have always claimed it would be much easier to be a parent if we were not human; however, if we were not human we could not provide a model of being human for our children.

To provide a working definition of "love," think: respect, recognition, appreciation.

Parents' Guide

Everybody deserves to be loved.

Everybody deserves to be loved. That includes and requires loving yourself, as I just mentioned.

Love may be unconditional, but relationship is not.

Love is often described as something that comes without conditions. No matter what does or doesn't occur, love does not cease, change, or require conditions to be met. However, the same does not apply to relationship. Love may be unconditional, but relationship is not. We all have needs within each of our relationships and we have the right to have those needs met. The whole purpose of relationship is to get needs met. I have a relationship with my publisher because I need to get my book published. I have a relationship with my neighbor because I need to have a safe and pleasant place to live. Naturally, each relationship looks different and has its own configuration of needs and conditions to be met. Relationships are a function of a set of needs unique to each relationship. It is our duty to our self to have those needs met. These needs are made known and met by the sensitivity of the other to our needs along with and enhanced by our ability to communicate these needs. The quality of any relationship is based upon the level at which the needs within that relationship are met.

So, it is not unreasonable of you or your teenager to get angry, impatient, or have feelings hurt in the midst of a relationship that includes unconditional love. The presence of those strong, unappealing feelings does not imply a lack of love or perception of love. Often it does include a lack of perception of

Because I Said So!!

love and the presence of these feelings often does suggest that a need/condition of that relationship is not being met.

You haven't blown it because you are angry, disappointed, even disgusted by your teenager. You haven't blown it because your teenager is angry, disappointed, even disgusted by you. We often question our love for or from another when we feel these ways and that may be looking in the wrong place for the deficit that may exist. Relationships have needs and it is your responsibility to make your needs known and to know the needs of you the other has.

Self-permission contributes to this particular end (loving yourself). **Self-permission** enhances every moment, if we permit it. If you give yourself permission to grow impatient with your child (this does not say, "…give yourself permission to be mean to your child because you feel impatient"), you are less likely to be mean to yourself and more likely to move past that impatience more quickly. If you give yourself permission to make a mistake (you will continue to make them regardless of how good a book this is and how good a student of this book you are), you are more likely to learn from the mistake, you are less likely to be mean to yourself, and more likely to move past that mistake more quickly.

"All you need is love" is similar to the idea that all a farmer needs is seeds and soil, water, air, sun, carbon, potassium, phosphorus, and nitrogen. A farmer can't be a farmer without those things (identified as "limiting factors" with regard to growing plants), but it takes much more than those things for a farmer to harvest a crop.

Parents' Guide

Love is a limiting factor. It is necessary, but not sufficient to successfully (defined as enjoying yourself and your teenager while equipping him/her to live through the choices he/she makes) raise a child. Self love and self knowledge, the identification of goals, the recognition of needs (yours and his/hers) within the relationship, the ability to communicate your needs and know your child's needs of you, and the ability to accept (you for who you are; he/she for who he/she is) help.

I just said that love alone is not sufficient and I stated other conditions that must be met, in my estimation, for successful child rearing to occur. However, I turn to my operational definition of love as the key to this success. I believe that if you feel respected, recognized and appreciated by yourself and honestly feel/think/know that you respect, recognize and appreciate your teenager and communicate the same, you will succeed at living through your child's teenage years. If you remember and practice these guidelines and measure your performance in these three areas (intra- and interpersonally), you will be all right. You might not know the "right" thing to do all the time, but you will know you are doing right by you and your teenager.

Two more things:

1) Notice, Remember, Repeat

What we notice we can remember. What we remember we can repeat. We humans are experts at noticing when we blow it, when we feel "bad" (angry, sad, afraid, disappointed, frustrated, lonely, and so on), and what makes us feel "bad." If that is all we ever

Because I Said So!!

notice that is all we can remember. If that is all we ever remember that is what we are bound to repeat.

If we begin to notice our good work (this includes not only our actions, but also feeling "good:" happy, satisfied, loved, confident, respected, recognized and appreciation by self; as well as how we come to feel these "good" feelings), we can remember this good work. If we remember this good work, when something (interaction, situation, problem) similar appears we can repeat this good work.

The above applies to yourself and you have a responsibility to help your teenager notice his/her good work, etc.

REMEMBER the two primary sources of power towards having things the way you want:

Knowing how good (not "good at" something) you are.

Keeping agreements with yourself as well as with others.

The better you get at noticing your good work, the better you will get at **knowing how good you are**; thus, making deposits in your "knowing how good you are" power bank towards having things the way you want. All good work includes agreement keeping. All skills improve with repetition. The more good work you notice, remember and repeat, the better you get at **keeping agreements**; thus, making deposits in your "keeping agreements" power bank toward having things the way you want.

Everything you do is for the payoffs; that is, having things the way you want; enjoying yourself, your

Parents' Guide

actions, and enjoying others and their actions; all the good feelings evoked by noticing your good work and the good work of others. The better you get at noticing these payoffs, the more payoffs you receive. **Everything you do is for the payoffs.**

2) *What we call our children, they will call themselves.*

Call your teenagers "stupid," "bad," "lazy," "smart," "beautiful," "capable," etc., and you will likely hear them call themselves that. How you describe them they will *notice*. Never underestimate the influence you have on your children.

Because I Said So!!
NEALISTIC SUMMARY:

One, Two, Three Cubed (1, 2, 3^3)

1. GOAL: To improve self-care (also known as "taking good care of ourselves"), which means:

   a) having a good time

   b) getting better at learning how our feelings affect our actions

   c) getting better at learning how our feelings and actions affect another

   d) getting better at learning how another's feelings and actions affect us

   e) identifying and sharing how we feel with those that care about us

2. We have two primary sources of power (to have things the way we want):

   a) Knowing how good we are.

   b) Keeping agreements with ourselves and with others.

3. We have three basic needs - respect, recognition, and appreciation.

   Respect - the acknowledgement of (I am)

   Recognition - the identification of (I am Neal)

   Appreciation - the valuation of (I am Neal. He is good.)

Parents' Guide

4. Improve my ability to notice, remember and repeat my own good work. What we notice, we can remember. What we remember, we can repeat. Developing an understanding and awareness of our basic needs will contribute to developing and tapping our two primary sources of power (to have things the way we want) that will result in improved self-care.

5. RULES:

   a) Do unto others as I wish them to do unto me, but I am not holding my breath (Golden Rule).

   b) Do unto myself as I wish others to do unto me (Platinum Rule).

   c) Be true to myself. Only when I do unto others, as I want them to do unto me can I ask them to do unto me in that same fashion. However, while I can ask I cannot expect.

   That is what I mean by "not holding my breath."

Teenagers' Guide

AFTERWARD

Thomas Jefferson once said: "I'm a great believer in luck and I find the harder I work the more I have of it."

GOOD LUCK!!!

www.ingramcontent.com/pod-product-compliance
Lightning Source LLC
Chambersburg PA
CBHW030332080526
44584CB00012B/828

What's the Big Idea?!

The Teenagers' Guide to the Teenage Years

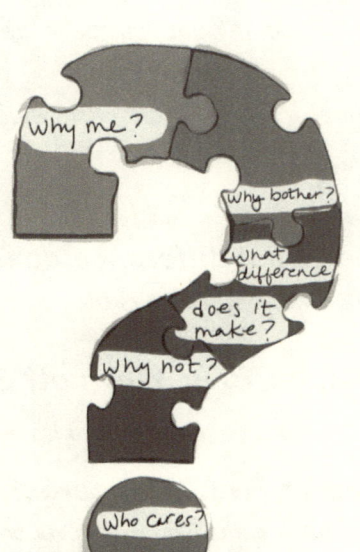

Table of Contents

Introduction: 3

Chapter One: *Why me?* 7

Our senses mediate our experience.

We act "as if" our perceptions are real.

Knowledge: justified belief

Do unto others as you would have them do unto you, but don't hold your breath.

Chapter Two: *Why bother?* 17

Be true to yourself...

*If you would sell out yourself,
you would sell out your best friend.*

Platinum Rule

Respect – Recognition – Appreciation

3R's

You are not your mistakes.

Chapter Three: *What difference does it make? 27*

*In every action or thought, there is the seed of its opposite.
The normal curve*

Chapter Four: *Why not? 33*

Drug use, not drugs, is the issue.

Chapter Five: *Who cares? 41*

Without acceptance, the work can never be complete.

What I don't know can't help me.

Everybody deserves to be loved.

Notice, Remember, Repeat!!!

Introduction

My friends call me G (short for Gee). I have been around for over 40 years, and my brother says that once you turn 40 and people tell you to grow up, you can say you have. So, I guess I have, though it doesn't feel that much different. When I was 11 or 12 or 13 years old (it's often hard to remember exactly – you'll see when you are 40) I got in trouble for doing something. I can't remember what it was (probably bouncing a ball off a wall or listening to my music too loud or something like that), but what I do remember is that what I was doing was just something any kid does. I wasn't being "bad," but I was treated as though I were. What irritated me was that if they (my parents, teachers) remembered what it were like to be 11 (12, 13) years old, they would treat us better. I swore I would remember on behalf of the kids I would encounter as an adult.

Well... did I mention I was over 40? Memory is not one of my strong points. I now find it difficult to remember exactly what it was like, so I can't actually keep that promise to myself or to today's teenagers (sometimes I'll call you "kids" – no offense intended). Since I can't remember, I will instead share with you what I have seen, tried, and thought since I was your age – reporting back to you like a scout reports back to his/her tribe. Here we go.

I believe that all of us spend all of our time and efforts towards having things the way we want – all day, every day.

3

What's the Big Idea?!

The two primary sources of power towards having things the way you want:

1) Knowing how good (not "good at ...") you are.

2) Keeping agreements with yourself and others.

This book includes 5 chapters. Each chapter can be read on its own or in any order. Each chapter addresses rules for action. A few good rules that can be generalized to fit different aspects of life work better than many rules for each. When I was 10 years old I noticed that refrigerators, washers, and dryers broke down and had to be replaced from time to time, but gas ranges never seemed to break. When I inquired why that might be, someone pointed out that a gas range has few moving parts (whereas refrigerators, washers, dryers each have motors), thus fewer things to break or to be replaced. That little piece of information provided me with an example I have tried to model in designing my life. This is not to suggest that I have any control over the unfolding of my life, but as it unfolds I attempt to act based on the few rules I will share with you in this book.

Think of this book as a guide, similar to a guidebook you might pick up in preparation for a trip to another land. Once you are there, chances are you will do whatever it is you like, but to prepare for the trip, reviewing another's experience of your destination may help you develop a plan of your own and keep you from making a few (though not all, I'm afraid) of the mistakes the writer of the guidebook made. The combination of considering others' experiences and making mistakes contributes to a successful journey (success is defined here as knowing more about yourself than when you began). If this book can serve you in that fashion, then I will have achieved my goal.

Teenagers' Guide

What's the Big Idea?!

Teenagers' Guide

Chapter One

Our senses mediate our experience.

We act "as if" our perceptions are real.

Knowledge: justified belief

Do unto others as you would have them do unto you, but don't hold your breath.

Our senses mediate our experience.

"What did he say?" you ask yourself. A whole lot appears to be going on around us all the time. We know (?? what do we really know? I'll come back to this point next) this by means of information being sent to our brain via our senses (vision, hearing, touch, smell, taste). We do not experience the world directly. Let me give you an example. Some of you wear glasses in order to improve your vision. Before you wore glasses the world may have looked fuzzy or distorted in some way. With the aid of corrective lens, the world now appears clearer, more detailed, and you feel a greater certainty as to what you might be looking at.

7

What's the Big Idea?!

Now take a look at this picture. What do you see? Is it a picture of an old woman with a shawl over her head or a young woman with a choker necklace and a feather in her hair? Which did you see first? Are you able to see both? Are you able to see either?

Did you ever play the game called "Whisper Down the Lane"? In this game, everybody in a group sits in a circle. One person decides on a sentence to pass around the circle by whispering into the ear of the person next to him/her, which gets passed to the next person in the same manner until it returns to the original sender. That person then shares the original message with the one heard after it traveled around the circle. Chances are that the two messages are significantly different. Why is this? I guess one possibility could be that someone chose to sabotage the exercise by making something up, but more likely each participant, having no cues but sounds whispered in his/her ear, reported to the next person what they thought they heard (or perceived). The editing that occurred in the process of each person's perception of the whispered message resulted in the creation of a whole new message by the time it completed its circuit.

"So what?" you say. "What the heck does this have to do with living my life in a fashion I choose? This is just more of that stupid stuff we always have to do as kids in health class, social skills groups, or mixers. How does this help me get

8

Teenagers' Guide

through the day?" Those are all good questions. Just hang in there and read on. I didn't become over 40 years old in a day.

One more thing regarding this first claim. There is an experiment where people observed a car accident and then reported what they witnessed. The researchers staged the accident, so they knew exactly what "really" happened. Only one in three of the witnesses accurately reported what had occurred, though they all told the truth as they saw/recalled it. If that is the case for an experience with the impact (pun intended) of an automobile crash, that is, people reporting their experience of it differently, then imagine how easy it is to misunderstand seeing our boy or girlfriend talking to someone, or not being invited to a party you wanted to attend, or not getting the job for which you applied?

Have you ever had the experience of reading a situation one way and learning later how others perceived it? When I was 21 years old, I hitchhiked across the United States with my girlfriend, Tamara, traveling from Pennsylvania to California. We stopped in Lawrence, Kansas to visit with her family. At the dinner table the night of our arrival sat Tamara's mother, father, two older sisters, a younger brother, and I. I noticed a few things like Tamara's Dad changing the subject immediately when I alluded to our hitchhiking together and brief moments of unexplained (to me) silence. Other than that I felt things had gone pretty well, and having been a little nervous about how things would go, I felt good.

9

What's the Big Idea?!

After dinner, all the "kids" hung out and compared notes on the dinner that we had all shared. The observations of Dad's behavior by all those who had been raised by him suggested to me that much more went on at that dinner table than I was aware of. Certain tones in Dad's voice, various expressions on his face, and some body language were totally lost on me due to my unfamiliarity with him as a person or a "Dad." Between the time dinner ended and the time we began our discussion reviewing the event, I had thought I knew what had occurred, but actually things had not gone as well as I had perceived. Suddenly my confidence in having been welcome and accepted by Tamara's father faded. I would not have done as well on a quiz about that meal as I had first thought before talking to his children.

We act "as if" our perceptions are real.

Now you may wonder, "If my perceptions mediate my experience of the world around me, how can I ever know what is 'really' going on?" Well, your wonderings (and all your feelings, for that matter) are real. We believe we know what the world around us offers. We know what we feel because we experience our feelings directly. We may not always understand our feelings or thoughts (oops! I should speak for myself – I do not always understand my feelings or thoughts), but we experience them without the use of our senses. We do not see, hear, smell, taste, or touch our feelings/thoughts. They come from within us. **All else comes to us through our senses, thus a step**

10

Teenagers' Guide

exists between what goes on out there and how we experience what goes on out there. In spite of that, we seem to manage and get ourselves through the day, some days better than others. If that is the case – that we cannot know what really happens "out there" – how do we do it?

The process of solving problems requires assessment first, or figuring out what is going on now; then intervention, or doing something to change what is going on. John Lennon (a member of that ancient rock 'n roll band, The Beatles) said it best (I rarely quote songs, but here goes) when he sung: **"How can I go forward when I don't know which way I am facing?"**

Knowledge: justified belief

A moment ago I claimed that we can never know what "really" goes on and now I claim that we cannot act until we assess. That leaves us in a position that requires us to act "as if" what we perceive is real. Or, we act based on our belief of what is happening. In fact, I read somewhere a definition for "knowledge" as being "justified belief." The example I use to help me understand this is the rising of the sun. I don't "know" that the sun will rise tomorrow, because it hasn't happened yet, but I make plans based on my belief that it will do so. Others would call this "knowledge" of the earth rotating on its axis once every 24 hours, but how do you know this? Spent much time out in space checking on the movements of this planet? Probably not,

11

What's the Big Idea?!

yet you act "as if" the sun will rise again tomorrow. The "knowledge" of this is a "justified belief." You cannot prove today that the sun will rise tomorrow, but that does not interfere with making plans.

I use this example to point out the role our beliefs play with regard to what we perceive goes on around us. That I know (believe?) I will never pass that test will influence how I approach the upcoming exam. If I know (believe?) I am good enough to make the team, this will affect how I perform. If I know (this may be an experience rather than a belief, or it may still be a belief) I am worth spending time with, I know (from past experience) I will live if I am rejected in my attempt to connect with another (never preferred but endurable). How I interpret how you treat me will affect how I treat you. And how I treat you affects the way you treat me which affects the way I treat you and on and on... That's why "they" call what we do with each other "interactions."

This claimed "knowledge" of how the future will unfold affects how it unfolds. Since our senses mediate our experience, we act based on how we interpret, or "as if." We have no choice but to perceive through the use of our senses and our interpretations of this incoming sensory input. I share the idea of "as if" to remind you of our relationship to the world around us; **that "real" to you may not always be "real" to someone else and your "real" is no more or less "real" than another's "real."** Recognition of this demands that you accept responsibility for your

Teenagers' Guide

interpretations. In many cases we may share interpretations (almost everybody agrees on the appeal of ice cream) and often we rely on social agreements to avoid differences in interpretation (we have all agreed to stop at a red light rather than to respond to it in our own unique way).

My interpretation of my dinner in Lawrence, Kansas, to which I referred earlier, differed from that of my sweetheart and her siblings. Until we compared notes later that evening, I thought my interpretation was "real." In our day-to-day lives there are few moments when we have the opportunity to compare notes with others, and regardless of how many others may be with us, our experiences are our own, resulting in the necessary interpretation (or perception), which we believe to be "real." The requirement to assess becomes clear; the recognition that this assessment is our own (even if shared by others) reminds us that these experiences are remembered by means of the interpretations we make.

1) Do unto others as you would have them do unto you, but do not hold your breath.

2) Be true to yourself ... but how do you want others to do unto you?

Chances are you have heard the part about doing unto others as you would have them do unto you. That always irritated me when others threw that up at me as a means of controlling my behavior. I always interpreted it to mean that I should sell myself out in order to "be nice," that

13

What's the Big Idea?!

when others take advantage of me I should just take it and respond in a polite, pleasant fashion. "Fat chance," I always said to myself. Seemed like whenever I sold myself out to keep everything pleasant and peaceful, I ended up holding the bag (holding the short end of the stick; taking it in the shorts; eating it; etc.).

Throughout my years of personhood I have observed a pattern with regard to my attempts to "do unto others..." What this expression refers to is the idea of modeling behaviors you wish others to exhibit, which is a great idea if it works. My understanding of the expression, "Do unto others as you would have them do unto you" includes the belief that I can ask nothing of someone else that I do not or will not do myself. That belief and the belief that expectations set me up for disappointment prompted me to add "...but don't hold your breath."

Whenever I expect another to behave as I do, I get nailed. I believe it important to be an example of the type of human being with whom I would like to share this planet. Now I still grow impatient, jump to conclusions, often think of only me, assume, feel sorry for myself, and so on. So, I must be prepared to see these behaviors in others. When I expect otherwise, I get burned. If you make appointments, you have disappointments.

"All right," you say. "For the sake of argument I'll consider the 'Do unto others...' baloney, but that helps me not at all when it comes to deciding how to act." Funny, that's exactly what I

14

Teenagers' Guide

said when trying to heed this unasked for advice throughout my days when I had to politely listen to adults attempting to modify my behavior (you and I have so much in common!). It turns out that this is the hard part, because our own judgment influences our actions and when it gets right down to it, the power to act (or not) is our own.

"Oh, great!" you say. "All this talk and now you throw it back into my lap. How do I make these judgments? How am I supposed to know what right or right action is?" An excellent question. Wish I had thought of it myself! The guideline I provide in order to help with this conundrum (one of my favorite words which means· a riddle difficult to solve) is: Be true to yourself. Quite a mouthful, you might say, but what do I mean? Chapter Two attempts to explain.

15

What's the Big Idea?!

Teenagers' Guide

Chapter Two

Be true to yourself...
but how do you want others to do unto you?

If you would sell out yourself,
you would sell out your best friend.

Platinum Rule:
Do unto yourself as you wish others to do unto
you.No matter how much or how many others
care for you, unless you care for yourself, there
is nothing anybody can do for you.

Respect – I am
Recognition – I am Gee
Appreciation – I am Gee; he is good

3R's
Respect for myself
Respect for another
Responsibility for my feelings and actions

You are not your mistakes.

Be true to yourself. ...but how do you want others to do unto you?

Okay, now where was I? Let's see: our senses mediate our experience; we act "as if" our perceptions are real; knowledge = justified belief; do unto others as you would have them do unto

17

What's the Big Idea?!

you, but don't hold your breath...; Oh yeah–be true to yourself. Thank you for your patience. At my age I get distracted easily. Okay, now where was I?

Platinum Rule:
Do unto yourself *as you wish others to do unto you. No matter how much or how many others care for you, unless you care for yourself, there is nothing anybody can do for you.*

So, you have heard this "do unto others..." crap before, you say, and it has helped you not at all in taking good care of yourself. Either you get taken advantage of when you try it or nobody appreciates it when you **"do unto others as you would like them to do unto you."** Not a lot of reinforcement for continuing this practice, eh? Well, I appreciate your position and for a long time held it myself until I stumbled across the second part of the expression that never seems to make it to the presses or out of the mouths of those claiming to provide us with guidance. **"Be true to yourself"** allows "doing unto others..." to work for you. The reason this part often gets lost is because it is the hard part and no one can do it for you. It requires a positive valuation of yourself. The better you feel about yourself, the easier it is to **"do unto others as you would have them do unto you."**

To feel good about oneself all the time does not come easy, particularly during one's teen-age years. Our bodies are often in revolt as we deal with puberty and physical maturation. We have to deal with: acne, developing later

Teenagers' Guide

(or sooner) than everybody else, voice cracking, tripping over our own feet, feeling different from everybody else, feelings we have never had before, moodiness, and changing tastes and desires. With our peers going through similar (yet unique to each of us) changes, we have to deal with: cliques, vacillating loyalties (now he/she is my friend, now he/she is not), popular styles you do not like, rejection (now he/she loves me, now he/she does not), and trying to keep up with what "cool" is at the moment.

To make matters even more difficult for "being true to yourself" we have our parents/foster parents/guardians and teachers, principals, and police officers telling us what to do, telling us how "bad" we are, telling us one thing and then another. They all claim they want to help us grow up and take care of ourselves, but it often seems to be only on their terms. Their idea of right for you is what they think is right for them and it often seems like they provide little acknowledgment of your feelings or thoughts on just about everything, which often compels you to do the opposite of what is advised simply because it is opposite (I call it the **"you can't tell me what to do"** reflex.). And even when you have responsibly thought out your position, adults rarely give you credit for it and if things do not work out, they interpret that as proof that they were right and you were simply being irresponsible. And then the icing on cake is the claim by adults everywhere, "do as I say not as I do" which is in direct

19

What's the Big Idea?!

contradiction with "doing unto others..." Then try pointing that out to them and it only gets you in trouble. Never a break, huh?

During my early years I held the belief that once I became an adult, all my problems would be resolved; the magic of adulthood would diminish my all too frequent impulse to cry; I would no longer be afraid of girls; and I would not have to be faced with all the jerks (adults and peers alike) I had to deal with daily. Though I feel more grown up than ever and will never be mistaken for a teenager, or even a young adult, ever again, I still cry often as control of that impulse eludes me; while I no longer fear girls, now it's women who scare me; and I still must face and endure others who irritate me and get in my way. The problems have not gone away and I still must face them day in and day out. Oh yeah, I also dismissed the myth that once an adult, things get easy.

Now, where was I? Being true to myself. Have you ever seen someone hurt themselves, or set themselves up, or get themselves in trouble in order "to protect" or "to help" a friend. A window gets broken by another kid, you get blamed and punished for it, and you stay quiet in order to protect this "friend."

You and a friend are both running for an elected office; you vote for your friend and you lose by one vote. If you choose not to vote for yourself, however, how can you ask anyone else to vote for you? You see your Mom across the street with hands full with bags of groceries.

Teenagers' Guide

In your interest in helping you hurriedly cross the street without looking and get hit by a car. How much use are you then to your mother? These examples help explain the importance of being true to yourself. While friendship is a valuable and necessary part of growing up among others, it does not provide an excuse for abandoning oneself. **You won't be much good to your friends if you ignore the responsibility of caring for yourself.** If you look out for your friend instead of looking out for yourself, and your friend looks out for him/herself, then two people look out for him/her and no one looks out for you. Uh-oh!! Where does that leave you? And what good are you to your friends if no one looks out for you.

If you would sell out yourself, you would sell out your best friend.

You heard me. I know and agree with the notion that loyalty plays an important part in a close friendship and I find no contradiction here. Though as you read this you may think I talk out of both sides of my mouth (also known as being "full of it"). I claim that we must be loyal to ourselves first and recognize that our friends are simply extensions of ourselves. If my friend has an alcohol or drug problem and I help him/her deny the problem (and/or help acquire the preferred substance) and risk getting in trouble myself out of "loyalty" to my pal, I place my friend ahead me, lending to the possibility that when I get in trouble, I cannot help my friend or myself – all under the pretense of "loyalty." **Your friends deserve to receive your friendship.**

What's the Big Idea?!

Until you make friends with yourself, you limit the friendship you can offer others.

Friendship. I seem to throw that word around pretty easily. I guess I ought'a take a moment to define what friendship provides. I have broken down friendship into 3 components: respect, recognition, and appreciation. "Oh great!" you say. "Take one word of which I think I know the meaning and turn it into 3 words of which I am less sure." (So, you've noticed my tendency to be wordy. You're not the first.)

> ***TO RESPECT*** *– to acknowledge*
> ***TO RECOGNIZE*** *– to identify*
> ***TO APPRECIATE*** *– to value*

Another way of defining these terms:

> ***RESPECT*** *– I am.*
> ***RECOGNITION*** *– I am G.*
> ***APPRECIATION*** *– I am G and he is good.*

In case you hadn't noticed, I used the first person (also known as "I") in defining these 3 components of friendship. This brings us back to the importance of caring for yourself the way you want others to care for you. **Unless I can respect, recognize, appreciate myself, I have little chance of showing respect, recognition, appreciation (friendship) toward another and less chance of being able to take it (friendship) in from others.**

Am I getting a little preachy? Well, it's my book. Please forgive me. I just remember all the lines fed me under the guise of demanding

Teenagers' Guide

my loyalty ("If you were really my friend you would..."; "Everybody else is doing it!"; "What are you, a baby?"). Need I go on? Friendship is valuable. Your friends are important. They deserve your friendship. Your friendship is valuable to your true friends. You are important to them. You deserve their friendship. However, please remember – no matter how much or how many others care for you and no matter how much or how many others you care for, unless you care for yourself, there is nothing anybody can do for you and little you can do for anybody else.

Please do not misinterpret the above to encourage self-absorption at others' expense. I, as your friend, rely on you to take care of yourself. There may be a time when I have to call upon you as a friend to help me. While I view you as a friend and only wish the best for you, I am so busy trying to get my act together that I must count on you to look out for you, to call upon me or others when you need help in getting your act together. The better shape in which you maintain yourself (physically and emotionally), the better you may serve me when I need a friend. Your acceptance of responsibility for yourself only makes you a more capable and attractive friend, which brings me to my 3 R's (another set of 3 simple, though not always easy, guidelines for serving yourself and your friends):

Respect for yourself.
Respect for others.
Responsibility for your actions and feelings.

What's the Big Idea?!

I have already defined respect above (acknowledgment of). Responsibility refers to the ability to respond or to be answerable. Many people choose to replace the term "responsibility" with the terms "credit" or "blame." I prefer the term "responsibility." If I do good work, I am responsible for it. If I do not do good work, I am responsible for that also. I am not "good" because I do good work (credit) and I am not "bad" because I do not do good work (blame).

If I score the winning basket at the buzzer of the championship basketball game, I am not good because I made the basket. I wouldn't have been on the court in the first place if I weren't good. Let them carry me off the court, but I was already good, not just because of my actions. If, instead, I miss the final foul shots after the buzzer and we lose that championship game, I am not bad because I missed those foul shots. As I said, I wouldn't have been on the court if I weren't good. I (and others) may be disappointed. But I am not bad because I missed those shots.

Think of the championship basketball game as our life. Think of us being on the court to participate in this championship game as us being born. **You will make mistakes. You will do great things (and it is those mistakes that will help you do those great things).**

You are not your mistakes.

I am always good, it is just that sometimes my actions and/or feelings do not meet my or others'

Teenagers' Guide

expectations. If I am good and I make a mistake or behave poorly, I have the capacity to do something about it. When I identify with my mistakes (when I believe I *am* my mistakes), I usually believe that mistakes are "bad." If I am my mistakes and mistakes are "bad," then...I am "bad." If I am "bad," then why bother doing anything about me? If I am "bad," then I cannot or am not worthy of correcting an earlier behavior or action, nor do I believe I am capable of making change. Having worked with kids and teenagers since I was a teenager myself, **I have yet to meet a bad kid.** I have met many teenagers who might disagree with me about being "good" kids and have met many whose behaviors may not be very appealing, and though I keep looking for my first bad kid, I have yet to meet him or her.

25

What's the Big Idea?!

Teenagers' Guide

Chapter Three

In every action or thought, there is the seed of its opposite. You can't have "on" without "off," "up" without "down," "good" without "bad."

The normal curve

In every action or thought, there is the seed of its opposite. You can't have "on" without "off," "up" without "down," "good" without "bad."

Let's talk (or rather you read, while I write) about this good/bad scene. Try defining "good" without using "bad". Try defining "up" without using "down." Try defining "on" without using "off." One defines the other. We call each of these pairs a "dichotomy – a division into two opposing parts." Each requires the other for clear definition. **Dichotomies help describe and explain the world. I am the world!!** We separate things from ourselves in order to understand ourselves. If there is only "I," then there is nothing from which to separate or to compare, or to relate to. However, that makes things difficult to measure, judge, or understand, and since my equipment (senses and thinking abilities) requires comparison and separation, I must separate myself (my view of my "self") from the rest of my perceived world as my means toward understanding myself and getting what I want.

27

What's the Big Idea?!

As I mentioned earlier, our perceptions mediate our experience of the world around us. We only act "as if" things are as we experience them. Dichotomies help us with measurement and judgment of these perceptions of our environment and ourselves. It appears that the human nervous system requires separation in order to understand. In the world of action and thought, within everything there is the seed of its opposite. One can't define "up" without "down," "in" without "out," "right" without "wrong."

We apply this same method to observing, measuring, and judging ourselves. But all we really "know" is only what we experience/perceive "now." We judge, measure, and observe in order to act. That assumes forethought with regards to our actions. I don't know about you, but I can claim little credit (though I remain fully responsible) for thinking about what I do before I do it as often as I would like. Generally I act upon impulse. If it's what I want to do now, I do it and consider the consequences of my actions only when they cause me pain or discomfort. If things go well or they don't make me uncomfortable, I ignore my process and assume I knew what I was doing. (Do you know the memory device for spelling "assume?" It makes an "ass" out of "u " and "me.")

Imagine you are in space and there is nothing else in space with you. Let's say you have the ability to move in space, even though there is nothing to push against. Now you move in

Teenagers' Guide

space. How fast do you move? Which direction do you go? How far do you move? Without a starting line, there can be no finish line, making it impossible to measure your distance, speed, or direction. Without separation, we cannot measure, compare, or judge, as I mentioned earlier.

Well, does that bring my claim earlier, "I am always good" into question? Maybe, maybe not. **More appropriately, I guess I should claim, "I am always" or just "I am." I am not good, bad, fat, thin, tall, short, smart, stupid, friendly, mean.** At any given moment, I and/or others may judge/perceive/measure me as such, but those reflect perceptions based on comparisons. And they change depending on a given action, thought or to what or whom I get compared. These are all "relative" terms.

If I compare my basketball ability to Michael Jordan's I judge myself as bad. Compared to other over 40-year-olds who like to play basketball, I probably would judge myself as average. Compared to all 40+ year-olds, I would judge myself as above average. If I compare my score on my Spanish final to what my father expects, I judge myself as bad. If I compare my score to an accurate reflection of how much I studied or cared, I might judge myself lucky. If I compare myself to how others did on this test I judge myself as average (I received a "C"). Do you begin to get my drift?

What's the Big Idea?!

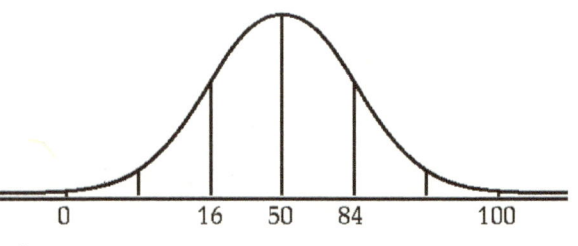

Normal curve

What you see above is called the "normal curve." This supposedly depicts the normal distribution of a population (or group). I learned about this in my first year of graduate school and wish that all of us were introduced to this idea in seventh and eighth grade. It helps me picture how and why things turn out when compared to others around me. Let's see if I can explain.

Let's say there is a perfectly symmetrical oak tree in your perfectly flat front yard. It is the middle of October and over the past week (when, incidentally, no wind or animals were present) this tree has dropped all of its acorns. Where do you think most of the acorns would land? Right!!! Most of them would fall close to the trunk of the tree. Not all of them would land there, however. The density of acorns on the ground would grow less as one moved away from the trunk. The farther away from the trunk, the fewer the acorns. And then you will always find a few that rolled even farther away when they hit the ground.

Think of 100 acorns falling from that tree and all of them have fallen between "0" and "100." Most of all the acorns fell between the "16" and "84."

Teenagers' Guide

Well, think of those fallen acorns as any group you care to think of. If 100 sixteen-year-old boys were each to eat as many pieces of pizza as they wanted in thirty minutes, most of them would eat around the same number (say, between 4 and 8 pieces), while some would eat more (9, 10, maybe one of them would eat 11 pieces), some would eat less (3, 2, maybe one of them would eat only 1 piece).

Please notice that I have begun to use terms like "most of them," "some," and "around." The purpose of introducing the idea of the normal curve is not to create a new generation of statisticians, but to provide a template (shape or pattern) through which you can observe in order to measure and compare in a fashion that does not imply good, bad, right, or wrong.

Important to remember: once you remove any part of a group, the normal curve must be reapplied to those that remain. If I compare my basketball ability to all 40+-year-olds, my ability will fall at a different spot on the curve (farther to the right) than if I compare my basketball ability to all 40+-year-olds who like to play basketball. If I compare my ability to all left handed 40+-year-olds who like to play basketball, or to all left- handed 40+-year-olds who like to play basketball and have beards, etc., my "spot" on each curve (representing different groups) will be different than my "spot" on the other curves. What you compare something with affects judgment or assessment or perception of whatever your are measuring. **It is all in how you choose to look at it.**

31

What's the Big Idea?!

Teenagers' Guide

Chapter Four

Drug use, not drugs, is the issue.

Chances are if you flipped through this book and saw this chapter heading, you turned to it first. Difficult to believe an old fart like me could have any idea how a teenager might think, huh? Well, I am glad to have gotten your attention. If you like this chapter, please go back to the beginning and read the rest. I worked as hard on them as I did on this one.

Mention the word "drugs" and it guarantees a rise of some kind no matter to whom you say it. Drugs!!! They are here to stay; from aspirin to alcohol to heroin. Face it. Drug use has saved countless lives. Drug use has destroyed countless lives. Drugs are not the issue. Drug use is the issue.

Out of respect, recognition, and appreciation for you I won't waste my breath and your time and effort by ranting at you about the dangers of drugs and tell you that you are bad if you take drugs (NOTE: any time I use the word "drug," that includes alcohol). However, I will ask that you consider the dangers of drugs (and alcohol) and **give yourself the respect, recognition, and appreciation you deserve.**

33

What's the Big Idea?!

Adults have a difficult time thinking about and discussing with kids drugs or sex because they always have to finish by saying, "Do as I say, not as I do" which they remember to be highly offensive when they heard it from adults when they were kids. I want to talk more about you and drug use than to talk about drugs.

If you have a bad infection you need to take antibiotics. Infection can kill. You banged up your knee or you have a terrible headache, you might take aspirin, acetaminophen, or ibuprofen. You have a sore throat and a bad cough, you might take cough syrup.

Now let's say you find yourself in a bad mood, your boy/girlfriend just broke up with you, your father just screamed at you, so you get drunk to help the pain and anger go away, right? Wrong!! Each of the examples I just cited includes a certain amount of risk in an effort to address the difficulty at hand. The antibiotics may kill the infection, but it also may upset your stomach and give you a case of diarrhea (am I allowed to use the word "diarrhea" in a book for adolescents?). The aspirin may reduce the swelling in your knee, but it might upset your stomach as well. The cough syrup may reduce your cough, but it may make you drowsy. Little we choose to do remains risk-free. Drinking alcohol or taking drugs to mend a broken heart, to deaden the anguish of abuse, to overcome depression ignores the cause of the pain and will provide short-term relief at best; not to mention the risks of breaking the law, losing friends, or having it affect your schoolwork.

34

Teenagers' Guide

Use of drugs for the reasons last stated introduces many and severe risks in exchange for the desired effects (Did you ever hear the expression, "The operation was a success and the patient died"?) Another metaphor might be "using a shotgun to kill a fly." Chances are you won't even get the fly, but you will leave one heck of a mess.

These metaphors do not address the unique quality of many drugs (alcohol in particular) known to have a high addictive potential. In a nutshell: this refers to the power a substance can acquire over an individual (any individual). Think of it as a merciless tyrant who will have things her/his way, at any cost. For adolescents and younger children the trail from repeated use to addiction can be a short one. You grow at such a rapid rate and have been humans for such a short time that drugs can overpower you without your awareness. This lack of awareness is often called "**denial**" (**which stands for: D**on't **E**ven **N**otice **I A**m **L**ying). That is... loss of respect, recognition and appreciation for yourself in exchange for serving a craving, meeting others' expectations (also known as "being cool"), or self-medicating ("When I drink, I do not fear talking to boys/girls/others.").

This pertains to adults as well as you all, but I m not writing to adults and you grow at a much faster rate than adults (being over 40 I am already beginning to shrink in height – hardly fast growth). Research has shown that where adults who become addicted to cocaine may take 6 months to 2 years from introduction

35

What's the Big Idea?!

before being in an addictive relationship with the drug, it may take as little as 6 weeks for a teenager to arrive at the same place.

Let me put it another way. You are at a stage in your life where you quickly tire of adults making decisions for you. You feel old enough and capable enough to make your own decisions. That remains a battle in which all generations must engage with their parents/guardians. So why sign up to have something else (a drug to which you are addicted, for example) make your decisions for you? That becomes a major risk of inappropriate, frequent, and/or dangerous drug use.

"All right," you say. "I agree with the idea that drugs/alcohol cannot help or heal emotional problems or scars, but I am just looking to party a bit. I feel good and just want to check out what intoxication is like. I'm not looking to solve anything, I am just curious and I have observed many people consume various substances with no ill effects. I just want to check it out!"

As I said earlier, I do not intend to yell at you or wag my finger at you or judge you poorly for these interests and impulses. I will tell you that it just scares the daylights out of me. I had the same impulses. I also had friends who were addicts and ruined their lives, others' lives, and sometimes died. I also have had friends who were not addicted to any substance, but their irresponsible use resulted in death. I used to work in a gambling casino at Lake Tahoe where alcohol, cocaine, and other drugs were common

Teenagers' Guide

commodities (alcohol in particular, once again). **During the nearly 4 years I resided in this beautiful resort area, I knew at least 1 person each year that either died or killed somebody due to alcohol or drugs in combination with alcohol.**

None of these people were bad people. I worked with most of them, hung out with some of them. I was in my mid-20s at the time which means most of my friends were also. **Those that died get to hang out no longer.** Those that lived and killed somebody (with a car in all instances) have to live with the knowledge that they exchanged another's life for the opportunity to become intoxicated through irresponsible use of drugs.

I still think of one friend, Ned (who I used to call Nedly), who used to like to stop by my place because we both liked to discuss what types of things we planned/wanted to do with our lives and our tastes in music were similar so we would exchange albums and talk about concerts we went to and wanted to attend. He and a friend (who lived) fell asleep while driving home from a party, where both did a considerable amount of drinking. Ned drove. When the other guy, Scott, woke up, he found himself in the car in a ditch on the side of a mountain road. It took him a moment to figure out what he was doing there, realized what must have happened, looked over to find Ned no longer capable of planning, doing or listening to music. **If you had spoken to either of them earlier that evening they would have assured you that nothing like that could happen to them.**

37

What's the Big Idea?!

So what is my point? My point is that it scares me to think about and to observe the risks kids take in order to become intoxicated ("get high," "catch a buzz," "turn on," etc.). If I knew that you had considered all possible risks (no easy task in and of itself) before choosing to indulge (that gives you the benefit of the doubt that you made a conscious choice rather than going with impulse or with the crowd), it would still scare me. However, being a human myself (though those that know me sometimes question that) I see in myself today and recall what I was like as a teenager the tendency to only see what I want to see and base my decisions on this hand picked data which I review to justify my interest in doing whatever I want independent of what is really going on or what real risks exist. So, it really scares me.

Rather than blathering further over my concerns about and the dangers of drugs and alcohol, I recommend you return to Chapter Two and review that blathering about respect, recognition, and appreciation and the 3R's **(Respect for yourself, Respect for others, Responsibility for your actions and feelings)**. My position states that a few good general rules serve us better than a slew of many rules that are specific to a particular situation.

However, the fewer the rules, the greater the responsibility of the follower of these rules to accept and to take the responsibility to gather and assess honestly all data that may be pertinent to a given decision. Remember, the decisions you make are yours. Regardless

Teenagers' Guide

of the outcome, you are responsible. Please look over these rules and see how they might apply to you and your choices with regard to your relationship with alcohol and drugs.

What's the Big Idea?!

Chapter Five

Without acceptance, the work can never be complete.

What I don't know can't help me.

Everybody deserves to be loved.

Notice, Remember, Repeat!!!

Without acceptance, the work can never be complete.

Tired of me yet? I thought so. Well, I am almost finished. When I began this scouting report I believed that I had much to say, but true to my claim at the end of the last chapter, good rules/ ideas preclude the need for many of them. And I would much rather you complain about the worthlessness of this book upon completion of it than not complete it because of its windiness (did I just make up a word?) or your inability to relate to anything I have written. So, just a few more things.

We could talk about all these guidelines I have suggested and have an interesting discussion about their value (or lack of value), keep it very abstract so we do not have to apply them to ourselves, and continue to

What's the Big Idea?!

go about our business in our unconscious fashion. I have already written about this in Chapter 2 so I won't repeat myself. I will just state it a different way in a much shorter fashion (you're welcome!). No matter how much you believe in improving yourself, care for yourself and your friends, or try to "do right," without acceptance of yourself and your friends, your goals remain difficult to accomplish.

In my training as a psychologist, they beat two things into my head: first assessment, then intervention. The more clear my understanding of what goes on in the present (assessment), what to do about it becomes clearer (intervention). That requires a minimum of editing of information about how things are and honesty with regard to accepting this information. Compared to looking at myself, this is a piece of cake. When the data do not apply to me, when I do not have to identify with all the problems, questions, uncertainties that make up this assessment, I have little difficulty accepting and not judging the individual and the experiences, decisions, and fruits of these decisions this individual brings with him/her. However, when I choose (or rather, attempt) to look at and to assess myself and my actions and the fruits of these actions, I quickly judge (blame/credit) and ignore and deny the stuff ("stuff" is a clinical term I learned in graduate school. I don't mean to talk over your head) with which I do not want to identify.

What I don't know can't help me.

Sometimes I think of myself as a large file cabinet filled with innumerable files. Many of them

Teenagers' Guide

I have easy access to and as a result I remain fairly familiar with them and have no trouble reviewing them and updating them as needed. There exist some files, however, that have an electrical charge connected to them so that if I ever attempt to open them in order to review them and/or update them, I experience great pain. As a result, I ignore them or even deny that they exist.

Unfortunately for me, they remain active files, in that they affect my life (though in some-times subtle ways) in ways that do not serve me (spelled· g·e·t·t·i·n·g w·h·a·t I w·a·n·t). No mat-ter how much effort I put forth toward keeping those other files current, my refusal/inability to enter these charged files keeps me from staying current. And like I mentioned above, without a complete and honest assessment, I cannot de-termine an appropriate and helpful (hopefully) intervention. In other words, unless I can ac-cept me for who I am, there is little I can do about me.

No easy task. I have a lifetime (at least) of per-sonal work ahead of me and my inability/unwill-ingness to accept all parts of me makes that work more difficult and less fruitful. The first step is to accept my unwillingness/inability to accept all parts of me. What I usually do is beat myself up (in a personal, un-public way) and jus-tify this self-abuse by proclaiming high standards for performance. You know, "spare the rod, spoil the child" and other garbage that excuses a lack of respect, recognition, and appreciation when one needs an excuse.

43

What's the Big Idea?!

We do not have to give up our realistic standards just because we accept that we may not yet meet them. Two important points in the last sentence:

1) Realistic standards:

This requires an honest and accepting view of what strengths, weaknesses, needs, fears, and judgments contribute to who we are.

2) We may not yet meet them:

Simply because we have not accomplished, achieved, completed, or even begun many of the things we feel we need to accomplish, achieve, complete, or begin does no mean they will/cannot occur. When I was 20 years old and dropping out of college (I returned later) I claimed I wanted to do this, and this, and this, and this, and this. I had not achieved, accomplished, etc. any of them and judged myself as entirely full of garbage, because of this apparent lack of output. Well, over 20 years later I find that I have done some (though not all) of those things in which I claimed interest. Some I did not because they were unrealistic, I changed my mind, or because I am still unwilling/unable to accept certain parts of me. However, because I did achieve/accomplish some of those claimed goals, I have given myself permission to continue making up more "this's." **And self-permission enhances every moment if we allow it.**

We all have a lot of work to do. The person next to you may appear to have his/her act to-gether, but be assured he/she has his/her own set of fears, judgments, and needs that make it

Teenagers' Guide

difficult to review and update all the files in each of their file cabinets. The first and ongoing step we need to take is toward the destination of accepting ourselves for who we are. Sure, there is work to do, but all we have is time. We can ignore and condemn ourselves instead, which is the path most of us choose most of the time, or we can begin to accept ourselves for who we are (so, maybe I won't make it in the National Basketball Association as a point guard. I can live with that, but I am not going to stop playing basketball).

Everybody deserves to be loved.

And that brings me to my last little reminder. **Everybody deserves to be loved.** No, fellas, that is not an acceptable line to use to try to get a girl to take off her clothes. It is the basis of life and growth. Chances are you have questioned whether or not you are lovable. You may have experiences in your life that suggest otherwise, but I hope we have spent enough time together that you trust/believe me when I say,

Everybody deserves to be loved.

Here's where my Platinum Rule comes into play: I must do unto myself as I would like others to do unto me. In order for me to do unto others as I would like them to do unto me, I must provide them with examples of how I treat myself as well as examples of how I treat others. Thus, *Everybody deserves to be loved by him/herself as well as by others.*

45

What's the Big Idea?!

Again, this takes us back to our primary responsibility, which is caring for ourselves. **Not just taking care of ourselves, but caring for ourselves.** We must grow to love ourselves before we can really experience another's love for us. I guess this is just another way of stating what I have written about throughout this little scouting report. Though it is a simple statement, not everything simple is easy.

Well, I think I have done it. This report is now complete. There is an expression that states, "You cannot tell someone something they don't already know." It took me a long time to understand that (proof that I couldn't hear it until I knew it for myself). Nothing I have reported to you is new or original. I hope that I have presented it in a fashion that you can use what you already know to help you become whomever it is you wish to become and to do whatever it is you wish to do. Until you get a taste of what I claim, these are only words on a page. So please consider, discuss, question everything I have written; if for no other reason than to humor an old man. To sum up:

1) You can do it! (whatever that "it" may be)

2) You are worth it! (no matter how harsh a judge you may be of your feelings and actions)

3) You are able to love and to be loved! (whenever you forget that, just ask me. I will tell you anytime.)

Teenagers' Guide

Oh yeah, one more thing (I really mean it, this time):

Notice, Remember, Repeat!!!

What we notice we can remember. What we remember we can repeat. We humans are experts at noticing when we blow it, when we feel "bad" (angry, sad, afraid, disappointed, frustrated, lonely), and what makes us feel "bad." If that is all we ever notice, that is all we can remember. If that is all we ever remember that is what we are bound to repeat.

If we begin to notice our good work (this includes not only our actions, but also feeling "good": happy, satisfied, loved, confident, respected, recognized and appreciated by self; as well as how we come to feel these "good" feelings), we can remember this good work. If we remember this good work, when something (interaction, situation, problem) similar appears we can repeat this good work.

If all we notice are our errors, poor choices, "bad" actions, then that's all we can remember. If that is all we remember, then that is what we are likely to repeat. **Our responsibility to ourselves requires that we notice our good work along with our bad work**. If we notice all of our work (actions, feelings, perceptions), we can remember them. If we only remember the bad, we have little choice but to repeat it. If we remember all of our work, we can use it to repeat the work that works and avoid or refrain from the work that doesn't.

47

What's the Big Idea?!

REMEMBER the two primary sources of power towards having things the way you want:

1) Knowing how good (not "good at ...") you are.

2) Keeping agreements with yourself and with others.

The better you get at noticing your good work, the better you will get at knowing how good you are; thus, making deposits in your "knowing how good you are" power bank towards having things the way you want. All good work includes agreement keeping. All skills improve with repetition. The more good work you notice, remember and repeat, the better you get at keeping agreements; thus, making deposits in your "keeping agreements" power bank toward having things the way you want.

Everything you do is for the payoffs; that is, having things the way you want; enjoying yourself, your actions, and enjoying others and their actions; all the good feelings evoked by noticing your good work and the good work of others. The better you get at noticing these payoffs, the more payoffs you receive. **Everything you do is for the payoffs.**

The stuff we repeat (practice) is the stuff we get good at. Only you can choose what to practice and only you can "make" you practice. Check it out. See for yourself. You deserve it!